THE WISHPOND LEAD GENERATION GUIDE

ANTHONY MALACHY

TABLE OF CONTENT

CHAPTER ONE

CHAPTER TWO

CHAPTER THREE

CHAPTER ONE
Understanding Lead Generation.

The process of locating and developing prospective clients (leads) for a company's goods or services is known as lead generation. Finding people who are interested in or in need of a company's products or services is the aim of lead generation, which aims to convert those leads into actual consumers. A range of strategies, including content marketing, email marketing, social media advertising, search engine optimization (SEO), and events or webinars, are often used to accomplish this. Businesses may grow their client base and income by generating leads.

Wishpond Lead Generation:

Wishpond is a marketing automation platform that provides a range of solutions for organizations to create leads. Some of the lead generating features given by Wishpond include:

Landing pages: Customizable landing pages that enable companies to develop a professional online presence and gather information from prospective prospects.

Forms: Drag-and-drop forms that may be used to take lead

information, such as names, email addresses, and other contact data.

Pop-ups: Customizable pop-up forms that may be used to gather lead information and enhance website conversions.

Contests and giveaways: Tools for hosting contests and giveaways to motivate lead generation and promote engagement.

Lead magnets: Digital products, such as ebooks, templates, and checklists, that may be supplied in return for lead information.

Wishpond also includes lead scoring, lead nurturing, and lead segmentation services to help organizations prioritize and manage their leads more efficiently.

Importance of Wishpond lead generation :

The lead generating capabilities of Wishpond may be crucial for organizations as they facilitate the collection and management of leads. Businesses can: by using Wishpond

Increase website conversions: Wishpond's landing pages, forms, and pop-ups are created to be aesthetically pleasing and conversion-optimized, assisting companies in gathering more lead information from website visitors.

Improve lead nurturing: Wishpond's lead scoring and segmentation tools let companies rank and group their leads according to their engagement and behavior, making it simpler to target them with relevant and individualized follow-up messages.

Save time and money: Wishpond automates many of the labor-intensive lead generating processes, allowing companies to concentrate on other aspects of their marketing strategies.

Success may be measured since Wishpond offers thorough analytics and reporting on lead generating performance, enabling companies to monitor their progress and spot potential improvement areas.

Businesses may more successfully engage with prospective consumers, develop connections, and expand their client base by using Wishpond's lead generating services.

Different methods and strategies that can be used to generate leads.

Landing Page:

On Wishpond, lead **generation with landing pages** entails building personalized pages that are intended to gather lead data and convert website visitors into leads. Here is how to accomplish it:

Decide on a template: Choose a landing page template from

Wishpond's collection of well crafted templates that complements your brand and marketing objectives.

Make the page your own: Edit the template to reflect your company's identity and include components that motivate website visitors to provide their contact information, such as forms, graphics, and text.

Optimize for conversion: To find the aspects of your landing page that convert well, such as headlines, pictures, and calls to action, use Wishpond's conversion optimization tools.

Publicize the page: To increase traffic and gather lead information, share the landing page on your website, social media platforms, or via email marketing.

Results tracking and analysis: Monitor the success of your landing pages and look for areas for improvement with Wishpond's analytics and reporting tools.

Businesses may utilize Wishpond to create leads and expand their clientele by developing high-converting landing pages and aggressively advertising them. Additionally, companies may continuously improve their landing pages to raise conversion rates over time by monitoring and evaluating their success.

Using competitions and giveaways on Wishpond to generate leads entails designing and publicizing a contest or giveaway that encourages website users to submit their contact information. Here is how to accomplish it:

Plan the gift or contest: Establish the contest or giveaway's rules and eligibility conditions, as well as the prize or benefits for participation.

Create the contest or giveaway: To create and personalize the contest or giveaway, use Wishpond's contest and giveaway tools, which also let you set up entry forms and rules pages.

Share the contest or giveaway on your website, social media platforms, and email marketing campaigns to promote it and increase traffic and lead generation.

Gather and manage leads: To save and arrange the lead data gathered from the competition or giveaway, use Wishpond's lead gathering and management capabilities.

Lead nurturing and email marketing solutions from Wishpond may be used to follow up with leads and persuade them to convert into customers.

Businesses may use Wishpond to create leads, cultivate connections with prospective consumers, and boost conversions by developing and marketing entertaining competitions and giveaways. Additionally, companies can efficiently prioritize and follow up with their leads to optimize the return on their investment by utilizing **Wishpond's lead management and nurturing features.**

Utilizing Wishpond's tools and capabilities to test and improve various aspects of your marketing campaigns can help you raise the proportion of website visits that convert into leads or customers. Here are some strategies for Wishpond conversion optimization:

A/B testing: To find out which of your landing pages, pop-ups, and forms generates the greatest conversion rates, compare them using Wishpond's A/B testing tools.

Lead scoring: Use Wishpond's lead scoring function to rank leads according to their engagement and activity so that you may target them with targeted and relevant follow-up messages.

Lead segmentation: Make use of Wishpond's lead segmentation function to classify leads based on their actions, passions, and demographics. Then, use this information to target them with relevant and individualized marketing messages.

Reporting and analytics: Make data-driven choices regarding your marketing plan by monitoring the effectiveness of your campaigns, identifying potential areas for improvement, and using Wishpond's reporting and analytics tools.

Landing page optimization: To find the aspects of your landing pages that convert best, such as headlines, pictures, and calls to action, use Wishpond's landing page optimization tools.

Businesses may successfully increase their conversion rates on Wishpond and optimize their return on investment by using these optimization tools and techniques. Additionally, organizations may continuously improve their efforts over time to provide even greater results by monitoring and evaluating their effectiveness.

On Wishpond, lead management entails utilizing the platform's features to gather lead data, store it safely, and then use it to forge connections and spur conversions. Here is how to accomplish it:

Create custom forms for collecting lead information, such as name, email address, and other pertinent facts, using Wishpond's form builder.

Integrate forms with campaigns: To guarantee that lead information is gathered properly and effectively, integrate your lead capture forms with your marketing efforts, including landing pages, pop-ups, and competitions.

Lead information, such as lead profiles, behaviors, and interaction history, may be stored and arranged using Wishpond's lead management features.

Use Wishpond's lead segmentation and scoring capabilities to score and classify leads based on their interaction and activity, and then target them with relevant and individualized follow-up messages.

Lead nurturing and email marketing solutions from Wishpond may be used to follow up with leads and persuade them to convert to customers.

Businesses may successfully acquire, store, and utilise lead information by using Wishpond's lead collecting and management capabilities in order to foster connections, encourage conversions, and expand their client base. Businesses can follow up with leads efficiently and increase their return on investment by using Wishpond's lead nurturing and email marketing solutions.

Pop-ups:

On Wishpond, pop-ups are a common method for gathering lead data. They are pop-up windows that show up on a website and ask users to provide their contact information in return for something useful, such a newsletter subscription, a discount, or a risk-free trial. Using pop-ups on Wishpond to generate leads is as follows:

Create a pop-up plan: A newsletter subscription, a discount, or a free trial are a few examples of what you could wish to provide in return for visitors' contact information.

Create the pop-up: To create and configure your pop-up, including the layout, text, and lead capture form, use Wishpond's pop-up builder.

Use Wishpond's targeting capabilities to target your pop-up and choose when and how it will display on your website, such as when a certain amount of time has passed or after a visitor has scrolled a specific amount of the page.

Organize and store the lead information that is gathered via your pop-up using Wishpond's lead management and collecting capabilities.

Follow up with leads: To follow up with pop-up prospects and persuade them to become clients, use Wishpond's email marketing and lead nurturing solutions.

Businesses can efficiently gather lead information, cultivate connections with prospective consumers, and increase conversions by employing pop-ups on Wishpond. Additionally, companies can efficiently prioritize and follow up with their leads to optimize their return on investment by utilizing Wishpond's lead management and nurturing features.

Email marketing:

On Wishpond, email marketing is a crucial tool for nurturing leads and increasing conversions. Businesses may develop connections with their leads and consumers, increase conversions, and send tailored and pertinent messages by using Wishpond's email marketing services. Here is how you utilize Wishpond for email marketing:

Segment your email list by activity, interests, and demographics to target leads with relevant and individualized email campaigns. Wishpond's lead segmentation tools may help you do this.

Create unique email templates using Wishpond's email template generator. These templates should reflect your brand's voice and tone of voice and should include the appropriate graphics, content, and calls to action.

Send targeted campaigns: Send welcome emails, nurturing programs, and promotional offers to your prospects and customers with Wishpond's email marketing tools.

Track success of email campaigns, including open rates, click-through rates, and conversion rates, using Wishpond's reporting and analytics tools.

Continuously improve: To get better results from your email marketing approach, use Wishpond's A/B testing and optimization tools to test various aspects of your email campaigns, such as subject lines, photos, and calls to action.

Businesses can efficiently nurture their leads, develop connections with their consumers, and increase conversions by using email marketing with Wishpond. Additionally, organizations may continually improve their email marketing approach to provide even greater results by using Wishpond's reporting and optimization tools.

Social media advertising:

On Wishpond, social media advertising is a potent tool for attracting new customers and generating leads. Businesses may develop and execute targeted ad campaigns on well-known social media sites, such Facebook, Instagram, and LinkedIn, utilizing Wishpond's social media advertising tools, in order to target their desired demographic. Using Wishpond's social media advertising is as follows:

Establish your target audience: To ascertain your ideal target audience, including demographics, interests, habits, and regions, use Wishpond's audience targeting tools.

Design ad content: Using Wishpond's ad builder, create personalized ad material that appeals to your target market and emphasizes the advantages of your product or service.

Set up ad campaigns: To decide on your ad budget, timetable, and targeting, as well as to set up your social media advertising campaigns, use Wishpond's ad campaign setup tools.

Measure and improve performance: To track the effectiveness of your social media advertising campaigns, including impressions, clicks, and conversions, use Wishpond's reporting and optimization tools. You can then improve your targeting and ad content to obtain better results.

Integrate with lead capture: To guarantee that lead information is gathered properly and effectively, integrate your social media advertising campaigns with your lead capturing initiatives, such as landing pages and pop-ups.

Businesses may reach new audiences, produce leads, and increase conversions by using Wishpond's social media advertising. Additionally, companies may continually improve their social media advertising plan to provide even greater results by using Wishpond's reporting and optimization tools.

Referral marketing:

On Wishpond, referral marketing is a potent strategy for generating leads and increasing conversions. Businesses may reward their customers and followers for referring their friends, family, and coworkers to their product or service by utilizing Wishpond's referral marketing tools. How to leverage referral marketing on Wishpond is as follows:

Set up referral campaign: To design and tailor your referral campaign, including the incentives provided to referrers and the procedure for doing so, use Wishpond's referral campaign setup tools.

Encourage consumers and followers to suggest friends and family by promoting your referral campaign via your website, social media accounts, email marketing, and other marketing methods.

Utilize Wishpond's reporting and analytics tools to monitor and evaluate the success of your referral campaign, including the volume of referrals, conversions, and income brought in.

Optimize and refine: To improve your referral marketing strategy's performance, test various aspects of your referral campaign, such as the incentive provided, the referral procedure, and the methods of promotion, using Wishpond's optimization and refinement tools.

Businesses may harness the influence of word-of-mouth advertising, reach new audiences, and produce leads and conversions by utilizing Wishpond's referral marketing tool. Additionally, companies may continually improve their referral marketing approach to provide even greater results by using Wishpond's reporting and optimization tools.

Event marketing:

On Wishpond, event marketing is a potent strategy for generating leads and increasing brand recognition. Businesses can organize and advertise events like webinars, seminars, and live events while reaching their desired audience by using Wishpond's event marketing services. Here's how to utilize Wishpond's event marketing features:

Identify the occasion's nature and intended audience: To decide what kind of event will most appeal to your target audience and the people you want to reach with your event, use Wishpond's audience targeting tools.

Make event material: To produce unique event content that appeals to your target audience and shows the advantages of your event, use Wishpond's event production tools.

Set up event registration: To set up and personalize your event registration process, including the registration form, registration page, and confirmation email, use Wishpond's event registration tools.

Event promotion: To reach your target audience, advertise your event on your website, social media pages, in emails, and via other marketing methods.

Gather and manage leads: Gather and manage lead data from your event participants, such as name, email, and contact information, using Wishpond's lead collection and management features.

Follow up and interact: Make use of Wishpond's follow-up and interaction features to interact with event attendees. This includes sending them thank-you letters, highlighting relevant goods or services, and enticing them to come to future events.

Businesses can reach new audiences, generate leads, and increase brand recognition by employing event marketing on Wishpond. Additionally, companies can effectively gather and manage lead information by utilizing Wishpond's lead collection and management capabilities, and they can follow up with attendees to encourage conversions and boost sales.

CHAPTER TWO
Implementing lead forms on Wishpond

One of the most important steps in the lead generating process is to implement lead forms on Wishpond. Businesses may use lead forms to gather lead data from website visitors, including name, email, and contact information. How to use lead forms on Wishpond is as follows:

Establish the aim of your lead form using Wishpond's goal-setting tools, taking into account the data you want to gather, the audience you wish to target, and the ultimate result of the lead form.

Create a lead form using Wishpond's tools, then personalize it with the fields you want to ask for, the form's look and feel, and the message that appears once you submit the form.

Place lead form on website: To place the lead form on your website, including on certain pages, blog posts, and other website places, use Wishpond's integration tools.

Lead form promotion: Encourage your audience to fill out the form by promoting it on your website, social media pages, in emails, and via other marketing methods.

Gather and manage leads: Utilize Wishpond's lead management and capture capabilities to gather and manage lead data from your lead form, such as name, email, and contact information.

Follow-up and engagement: Use Wishpond's options for follow-up and engagement to interact with leads, including by sending them thank-you letters, highlighting relevant goods or services, and guiding them toward conversion.

Businesses may use Wishpond's lead forms to gather lead information from website visitors, follow up with leads to encourage conversions, and boost sales. Additionally, companies can effectively manage and monitor the efficacy of their lead forms and continually improve their lead generating strategy by using Wishpond's lead management tools.

how to create lead forms that are easy to use:

Below are some guidelines for designing user-friendly lead forms:

Keep it brief and straightforward; just request necessary details.

Make sure the form fields are labeled simply and succinctly so that users understand what information is being asked.

Employ visual cues: To keep users interested, highlight necessary fields or display progress indicators.

Make it mobile-friendly by optimizing the form for smartphones, which account for a major amount of current online traffic.

Give precise instructions: For each field, include succinct explanations or examples to assist users understand what data is required.

Test the form: To find any obstacles or places for improvement, test the form with actual users.

Offer immediate validation: Let users know right away if they've made a mistake or if any necessary fields are missing.

Think about utilizing a form builder: To construct forms fast and efficiently, think about using a form builder that offers pre-made templates and drag-and-drop capability.

These suggestions can help you develop lead forms that are simple to use and promote greater conversion rates.

CHAPTER THREE

Marketing your lead magnet.

You may use the following procedures to promote your lead magnet on Wishpond:

Create a landing page: Make a visually attractive page with your lead magnet and a signup form using Wishpond's landing page builder.

Ensure that your page is search engine optimized by incorporating pertinent keywords and meta descriptions.

Drive traffic to the page: Use a range of channels, including as paid advertising, social media, and email marketing, to drive visitors to the landing page.

Provide a perk: Provide subscribers with a perk for joining up, such as a discount, access to premium material, or early access to a new product.

Use email marketing to follow up with users who have signed up and to distribute your lead magnet.

Monitor your progress: Track the performance of your marketing campaign with Wishpond's analytics and reporting tools and spot areas for improvement.

These techniques will help you promote your lead magnet on

Wishpond and develop your email list.

importance of tracking and analyzing your lead generation results:

It's crucial to track and evaluate your lead generating outcomes since doing so enables you to:

How to evaluate the success of your campaigns: You may identify the campaigns that are most successful and make data-driven judgments about the approaches to invest in by keeping track of the number of leads produced.

Enhance your approach: You may find areas for improvement and improve your lead generating strategy by evaluating the data.

Effective resource allocation requires knowledge of the expenses related to each lead. With this knowledge, you can distribute your resources in the best possible way.

Identify high-performing channels: By keeping track of where each lead comes from, you can figure out which channels are producing the highest-quality leads and focus more of your resources there.

Enhance the customer experience: You may find areas where the customer experience can be enhanced, leading to increased conversion rates and customer loyalty, by monitoring customer feedback and interaction.

Make data-driven choices: By having a thorough knowledge of your lead generation outcomes, you can choose your marketing plan with more data-driven accuracy and increase your return on investment.

In general, monitoring and evaluating your lead generation results is essential for determining the efficacy of your campaigns, enhancing your approach, and making defensible choices to enhance your outcomes.

Different metrics that can be used to measure Lead generation success:

Lead Volume:

Lead volume is a statistic used in lead generation efforts that counts all the leads produced during a certain campaign or over a predetermined time frame. It offers a broad overview of a campaign's effectiveness in terms of the quantity of produced leads or prospective consumers. Lead volume is a crucial indicator for assessing the success of a lead generation campaign and may assist companies in choosing the right investment strategies based on data.

Conversion rate:

The conversion rate is a statistic used in lead generation that assesses the proportion of site visitors who complete a desired activity, including submitting a form, making a purchase, or downloading a resource. It illustrates how well a lead generation campaign converts site visitors into leads or customers.

By dividing the total number of conversions by the total number of visits and multiplying by 100, the conversion rate is determined. As an example, a landing page's conversion rate would be 100/1000 or 10% if 100 visitors filled out the form.

As it directly affects a campaign's performance, increasing conversion rates is a crucial objective in lead generation. Businesses may improve the possibility that visitors will turn into leads or customers by improving landing pages, website design, and call-to-action components. Businesses may also pinpoint areas for improvement and make data-driven choices to gradually boost their conversion rates by monitoring and evaluating conversion rates.

Cost per lead (CPL)

Cost per lead (CPL) is a metric used in lead generation to measure the cost of acquiring each lead. It is calculated by dividing the total cost of a lead generation campaign by the number of leads generated. The CPL metric is important for determining the effectiveness and efficiency of a lead generation campaign and for allocating resources effectively.

For example, if a lead generation campaign costs $1000 and

generates 100 leads, the CPL would be $10 ($1000 / 100 leads). A lower CPL indicates that a campaign is more cost-effective in terms of acquiring leads, while a higher CPL may indicate that the campaign is less efficient and may need to be optimized.

By tracking and analyzing CPL, businesses can make data-driven decisions about their lead generation strategy, such as adjusting their budget, refining their targeting, or adjusting their tactics, to achieve a more favorable CPL and improve their return on investment.

Engagement rate:
A statistic for measuring the degree of interaction and engagement with a lead

generation campaign is the engagement rate. It may include activities like clicking on a call-to-action, opening and clicking on an email campaign, or staying on a landing page for a certain amount of time. The success of a campaign in grabbing and retaining prospects' attention may directly affect conversion rates, as seen by the engagement rate.

By dividing the total number of engagement activities by the total number of impressions or delivered campaigns and multiplying by 100, the engagement rate is determined. The engagement rate, for instance, would be 10% (100 / 1000 * 100) if a campaign email was sent to 1000 recipients and 100 recipients clicked on a call-to-action.

In order to better understand the interests and demands of their target market and increase the likelihood that prospects will become leads or customers, firms should strive to increase engagement rates. Businesses may discover areas for development and make data-driven choices to raise their engagement rates over time by monitoring and evaluating engagement rates.

Return on investment (ROI):

In terms of lead generation, ROI (Return on Investment) refers to the computation of the financial gain or loss resulting from a lead generation activity or campaign in relation to the cost of such initiative. In terms of the monetary return produced, it aids in gauging the success and efficiency of lead generating operations. ROI is calculated as follows:

(Leads produced revenue - Lead generation expense) / Lead generation expense.

In most cases, the outcome is reported as a percentage, with a positive percentage denoting a successful investment and a negative percentage denoting a failure.

Lifetime value of a customer (LTV):

In lead generation, a customer's lifetime value (LTV) is the expected sum of money they will spend on a business's goods or services over the length of their association with the business. It is used to assess a client's worth to a company and aids in setting priorities and allocating resources for lead generation and customer acquisition initiatives. The LTV formula is:

LTV is calculated as Average Revenue per Customer times Average Customer Lifetime.

LTV helps organizations evaluate the most they can spend on gaining a new client while still being profitable by measuring the possible return on investment for lead generation initiatives. Understanding LTV enables businesses to manage resources wisely and decide on lead generation techniques that will optimize the long-term value of their client base.

www.ingramcontent.com/pod-product-compliance
Lightning Source LLC
Chambersburg PA
CBHW071148240526
45465CB00024BA/1997